Table of Contents

Introduction... 1
Chapter 1: Introduction to Nutrition Coaching.. 7
Chapter 2: Assessing Your Skills and
Qualifications.. 11
Chapter 3: Understanding Your Target Market.14
Chapter 4: Developing Your Business Plan..... 18
Chapter 5: Legal and Regulatory
Considerations.. 23
Chapter 6: Setting Up Your Business
Operations.. 27
Chapter 7: Building Your Brand and Online
Presence... 37
Chapter 8: Acquiring Clients and Networking. 42
Chapter 9: Providing Exceptional Service........ 47
Chapter 10: Growing Your Nutrition Coaching
Business.. 52

Introduction

The Ultimate Guide on How to Start a Nutrition Coaching Business

Starting a nutrition coaching business can be an incredibly fulfilling journey. Imagine being able to help others lead healthier lives, reach their wellness goals, and feel their best. If you're passionate about nutrition and have the expertise to guide others, then this might be the perfect venture for you. But where do you start? How do you turn your passion into a thriving business? Let's dive into the steps you need to take to make your dream a reality.

1. Assess Your Qualifications and Skills

Before anything else, it's crucial to assess your qualifications and skills. Do you have a degree in nutrition, dietetics, or a related field? Are you a certified nutritionist or dietitian? If not, you might want to consider obtaining a certification from a reputable organization. This not only boosts your credibility but also ensures you have the necessary knowledge to provide effective guidance.

Additionally, think about your interpersonal skills. Being a nutrition coach is not just about knowing what to eat; it's about being able to communicate effectively, empathize with clients, and motivate them. If you feel you could improve in these areas, consider taking courses or attending workshops to enhance your skills.

2. Understand Your Target Market

Who are you going to help with your nutrition coaching? Understanding your target market is key to tailoring your services to meet their needs. Are you focusing on athletes, busy professionals, parents, or perhaps individuals with specific health conditions like diabetes or heart disease?

Research your potential clients' needs, preferences, and pain points. This information will help you design your programs and market your services effectively. For instance, busy professionals might appreciate meal planning tips that save time, while athletes might be more interested in optimizing their diet for performance.

3. Develop Your Business Plan

A solid business plan is essential for any successful business. It acts as a roadmap, guiding you through the initial stages and helping you stay on track as you grow. Your business plan should include:

- **Mission Statement:** Why are you starting this business? What do you hope to achieve?
- **Services Offered:** Outline the services you will provide. Will you offer one-on-one coaching, group sessions, online courses, or meal planning services?
- **Market Analysis:** What does the competitive landscape look like? Who are

your competitors, and what can you do differently?
- **Marketing Strategy:** How will you attract clients? Think about both online and offline strategies.
- **Financial Plan:** Estimate your startup costs, pricing strategy, and financial projections for the first few years.

4. Set Up Your Business Operations

Now it's time to get down to the nitty-gritty of setting up your business operations. This includes:

- **Choosing a Business Name:** Pick a name that reflects your brand and is easy to remember.
- **Registering Your Business:** Depending on your location, you might need to register your business with the local government.
- **Setting Up Your Workspace:** Decide whether you'll work from home, rent an office space, or offer virtual coaching.
- **Creating a Website:** A professional website is crucial for attracting clients and showcasing your services. Include information about your background, services, pricing, and contact details.
- **Legal Considerations:** Ensure you have the necessary licenses and insurance to operate legally.

5. Build Your Brand and Online Presence

Your brand is what sets you apart from the competition. It's how you communicate your values, mission, and services to your potential clients. Start by creating a logo and choosing a color scheme that reflects your brand's personality.

Next, focus on building your online presence. Social media platforms like Instagram, Facebook, and LinkedIn are great for reaching potential clients. Share valuable content like nutrition tips, success stories, and healthy recipes. Engage with your audience by responding to comments and messages promptly.

6. Market Your Services

Marketing is all about getting the word out about your business. Here are some strategies to consider:

- **Content Marketing:** Write blog posts, create videos, or start a podcast to share your expertise and attract potential clients.
- **Email Marketing:** Build an email list and send regular newsletters with valuable content and updates about your services.
- **Networking:** Attend local health and wellness events, join professional organizations, and connect with other health professionals who might refer clients to you.
- **Partnerships:** Partner with gyms, wellness centers, or even local businesses to offer joint promotions.

7. Provide Exceptional Client Service

Once you start attracting clients, the focus shifts to providing exceptional service. This is what will set you apart and lead to repeat business and referrals. Here are some tips:

- **Personalize Your Approach:** Tailor your advice and plans to each client's unique needs and goals.
- **Be Supportive:** Offer encouragement and celebrate your clients' successes, no matter how small.
- **Stay Educated:** The field of nutrition is always evolving. Stay up-to-date with the latest research and trends to provide the best possible advice.
- **Collect Feedback:** Regularly ask for feedback to understand what's working and what could be improved.

8. Grow Your Business

As you gain more clients and experience, you can start thinking about ways to grow your business. This might include:

- **Expanding Your Services:** Consider adding new services like cooking classes, workshops, or retreats.
- **Hiring Staff:** If you're overwhelmed with clients, it might be time to hire additional coaches or administrative support.
- **Scaling Online:** Offer online courses or membership programs to reach a wider audience.

- **Investing in Marketing:** As your budget allows, invest in paid advertising to attract more clients.

Final Thoughts

Starting a nutrition coaching business is a journey that requires dedication, passion, and a lot of hard work. But with the right preparation and mindset, it can also be incredibly rewarding. You'll have the opportunity to make a real difference in people's lives while building a business you love. So take that first step, stay committed, and watch your dream come to life.

Chapter 1: Introduction to Nutrition Coaching

Welcome to the exciting world of nutrition coaching! If you're passionate about health and wellness, and you're looking for a career where you can make a real difference in people's lives, then you're in the right place. Nutrition coaching is more than just a job—it's a way to help others achieve their health goals and improve their quality of life. In this chapter, we'll explore what nutrition coaching is all about and why it's become such an important field in today's society.

What is Nutrition Coaching?

So, what exactly is nutrition coaching? At its core, nutrition coaching involves guiding individuals or groups towards healthier food choices and a more balanced approach to eating. It's not just about handing out diet plans and meal suggestions. Instead, it's about helping your clients develop a positive relationship with food and understand the crucial role nutrition plays in their overall health and wellness.

As a nutrition coach, you'll work closely with your clients to assess their current eating habits, identify areas for improvement, and create personalized plans that cater to their specific needs. Your job is to provide ongoing support, education, and motivation, helping individuals make long-lasting changes and achieve their optimal health outcomes.

The Importance of Nutrition Coaching

In today's fast-paced world, where convenience often trumps nutrition, maintaining a healthy diet can be a real challenge for many people. The rise in chronic diseases like obesity, diabetes, and heart disease underscores the need for effective nutrition interventions. This is where nutrition coaching comes into play.

Nutrition coaching is a vital tool in addressing these health concerns and promoting preventive healthcare. By working with a nutrition coach, individuals can access expert advice and evidence-based strategies to improve their overall well-being. Nutrition coaches help clients understand their unique nutritional needs, set realistic goals, and make sustainable changes in their eating habits. Essentially, they empower people to take control of their health and make informed decisions about their diet.

The Role of a Nutrition Coach

As a nutrition coach, you'll wear many hats. You'll be a mentor, educator, and motivator all rolled into one. Your deep understanding of nutrition science, current research, and dietary guidelines will be your foundation as you guide your clients towards healthier eating habits.

Your role doesn't stop at providing nutritional guidance. You'll also help your clients overcome barriers and challenges they might face along the way. Whether it's offering personalized support, holding them accountable, or providing that extra bit of encouragement, you'll be there to help them stay on track and achieve sustainable results. Sometimes, you'll collaborate with other healthcare professionals, like doctors and dietitians, to ensure your clients receive comprehensive care.

The Benefits of Becoming a Nutrition Coach

If you have a passion for helping others and a strong interest in nutrition, a career as a nutrition coach can be incredibly fulfilling. Imagine the joy of making a positive impact on someone's life, helping them achieve their health goals, and seeing them thrive. That's the kind of satisfaction you can look forward to as a nutrition coach.

Not only is the work rewarding, but it also offers plenty of opportunities for professional growth and financial success. As a nutrition coach, you have the flexibility to work in various settings—fitness centers, wellness clinics, or even your private practice. You can choose to work one-on-one with clients, lead group workshops, or develop online programs to reach a broader audience. The demand for qualified nutrition coaches is on the rise, giving you ample opportunities to build a successful business around your passion.

In the upcoming chapters, we'll dive deeper into the different aspects of starting and running a nutrition coaching business. You'll learn how to assess your skills and qualifications, understand your target market, develop a business plan, navigate legal and regulatory considerations, set up your business operations, build your brand and online presence, acquire clients through effective networking, provide exceptional service, and ultimately grow your nutrition coaching business.

So, let's move on to Chapter 2 and start exploring the first steps towards building your successful nutrition coaching career. Stay tuned for Chapter 2: Assessing Your Skills and Qualifications.

Chapter 2: Assessing Your Skills and Qualifications

Starting a nutrition coaching business is an exciting venture, but before diving in, it's essential to take a step back and assess your skills and qualifications. This process helps you understand your strengths, identify areas where you might need improvement, and determine how you can create a successful and effective coaching practice. Let's walk through this together.

Identifying Your Skills

First things first, let's reflect on what you already bring to the table. Think about your formal education. Do you have a degree in nutrition or a related field? Have you completed any certifications or professional courses that bolster your knowledge? These academic credentials are the backbone of your coaching practice, giving you the necessary theoretical foundation.

But education is just one piece of the puzzle. Practical experience is equally important. Have you worked in health or wellness-related roles before? This could be anything from a job at a fitness center to a position in a healthcare facility, or even volunteering. Real-world experience not only boosts your credibility but also provides valuable insights into the challenges and needs your clients might face.

Next, consider your interpersonal and communication skills. These are crucial for building trust and effectively conveying your knowledge. Are you a good listener? Can you explain complex nutrition concepts in a way that's easy to understand? These skills are vital for motivating and guiding your clients toward healthier choices.

Recognizing Areas for Improvement

After you've identified your strengths, it's time to take an honest look at areas where you might need some improvement. Are there gaps in your knowledge or skills specific to nutrition coaching? Maybe there's a particular aspect of nutrition science you're not as familiar with, or a coaching technique you haven't mastered yet.

Continuing education is your best friend here. Look into courses, workshops, or conferences that can help you fill these gaps. You might also consider finding a mentor – someone experienced in the field who can offer guidance and share their expertise.

Staying up-to-date with the latest research and trends in nutrition is also critical. Make it a habit to read scientific literature, subscribe to reputable nutrition journals, and follow industry experts on social media. This ongoing learning ensures that your recommendations are always based on the most current and reliable information.

Seeking Professional Recognition

Professional recognition can significantly enhance your credibility as a nutrition coach. Certification programs from reputable organizations like the National Academy of Sports Medicine (NASM), the International Society of Sports Nutrition (ISSN), or the National Association of Nutrition Professionals (NANP) are great options. These certifications not only validate your expertise but also offer ongoing education and networking opportunities.

Be aware that certification requirements can vary depending on where you live. Make sure to familiarize yourself with the regulations and licensing requirements in your area to ensure you're fully compliant.

Conclusion

Assessing your skills and qualifications is a vital step in starting your nutrition coaching business. By understanding your strengths, recognizing where you need to grow, and seeking professional recognition, you position yourself as a knowledgeable and competent coach. Remember, the field of nutrition is always evolving, so continuous learning and personal growth are key.

In the next chapter, we will explore how to understand your target market. This knowledge will help you tailor your services to meet the specific needs of your clients, setting the stage for a thriving coaching practice. Stay tuned!

Chapter 3: Understanding Your Target Market

Hey there! So, you're diving into the world of nutrition coaching, huh? That's awesome! One of the first and most crucial steps to kick-starting and running a successful nutrition coaching business is really understanding who your target market is. But what does that mean, exactly? Your target market is basically that specific group of people or organizations you plan to serve with your awesome nutrition coaching services. By getting a good grasp on their needs, preferences, and challenges, you can tailor your approach and effectively market your services to them. Sounds important, right? Let's break it down together.

Why is Understanding Your Target Market So Important?

Understanding your target market is like having a superpower. It lets you create a laser-focused and super effective marketing strategy. When you know who your ideal clients are, you can craft your messaging and services to really hit home with them. This boosts your chances of attracting and keeping clients who are genuinely interested in what you offer. Plus, it saves you time and money because you're not trying to be everything to everyone. Instead, you're speaking directly to those who need and want your help.

How to Identify Your Target Market

So, how do you go about identifying your target market? Here are some steps to get you started:

1. **Research the Demographics** Start by digging into the demographics of your potential clients. Think about factors like age, gender, income level, and where they live. This information will help you narrow down and define exactly who your target market is. For example, are you aiming to help busy professionals in their 30s and 40s who live in urban areas? Or maybe you're focusing on young athletes looking to improve their performance? The more specific you can get, the better.
2. **Identify Specific Needs and Goals** Next up, figure out what specific needs and goals your target market has when it comes to nutrition coaching. Are they looking to lose weight? Manage a chronic condition? Boost their athletic performance? Or maybe just improve their overall wellness? By understanding what they want to achieve, you can tailor your services to meet their unique needs.
3. **Conduct Market Research** Market research is your best friend here. Use surveys, interviews, or focus groups to gather information about your potential clients' preferences, challenges, and motivations. You can also look at existing data and trends in the nutrition and wellness industry to get a broader sense of what's going on. This step is all about getting to

know your potential clients on a deeper level.
4. **Analyze the Competition** Don't forget to check out the competition. Who else is serving your target market? What are they doing well, and where are they falling short? Understanding your competition helps you find ways to differentiate your services and pinpoint a unique selling point for your business. This way, you can stand out in the crowd.

Creating Buyer Personas

Once you've gathered all this great information about your target market, it's time to create buyer personas. What are those, you ask? Buyer personas are fictional representations of your ideal clients based on real data and market research. They help you visualize and understand the motivations, needs, and challenges of different segments within your target market.

When creating your personas, consider factors like age, lifestyle, dietary preferences, and motivations. For example, one persona might be "Busy Brenda," a 35-year-old professional who wants quick, healthy meal plans to fit her hectic schedule. Another could be "Fitness Frank," a 25-year-old athlete looking to enhance his performance with optimal nutrition. Having these personas in mind will allow you to tailor your marketing messages and services to cater to the specific needs and preferences of each group.

Refining Your Target Market

As you get your nutrition coaching business off the ground, remember that understanding your target market is an ongoing process. Keep refining and adjusting based on feedback and insights from your clients. Your understanding of your target market will evolve as your business grows and you gain more experience. Stay flexible and open to change.

Conclusion

In the end, understanding your target market is absolutely essential for the success of your nutrition coaching business. By identifying their needs, goals, and preferences, you can tailor your approach and market your services effectively. Conduct thorough research, analyze your competition, and create detailed buyer personas to guide your efforts. And remember, this is an ongoing process – keep refining your understanding as you grow. With these steps, you're well on your way to building a thriving nutrition coaching business that truly resonates with your clients. Happy coaching!

Chapter 4: Developing Your Business Plan

Developing a business plan is one of the most crucial steps in starting and running a successful nutrition coaching business. Think of it as your business's blueprint, outlining your goals, strategies, and financial projections. It's a tool that provides clear direction and helps you make informed decisions as you navigate the journey of entrepreneurship.

Why is a Business Plan Important?

A business plan isn't just a document to show potential investors or lenders; it's a strategic tool that offers numerous benefits:

1. **Define Your Business:** A business plan allows you to clearly define your nutrition coaching business. It helps you articulate your mission, vision, and values, and identify your unique selling proposition and competitive advantage.
2. **Set Goals and Objectives:** By setting specific, measurable, achievable, relevant, and time-bound (SMART) goals, you can track your progress and stay focused on what matters most. These goals serve as milestones on your path to success.

3. **Identify Target Market:** Your business plan helps you pinpoint your target market, understand their needs and preferences, and tailor your services and marketing efforts accordingly. Knowing your audience is key to offering services that resonate with them.
4. **Analyze Competition:** A thorough analysis of your competitors is essential. It helps you identify gaps in the market and understand how to differentiate your business. Knowing your competitors' strengths and weaknesses allows you to position yourself more effectively.
5. **Develop Marketing and Sales Strategies:** Your business plan should outline your marketing and sales strategies, including pricing structure, target audience, advertising channels, and promotional activities. This ensures you have a clear plan for attracting and retaining clients.
6. **Financial Projections:** A well-crafted business plan includes financial projections such as startup costs, operating expenses, revenue forecasts, and profit margins. These projections help you understand the financial viability of your business and can attract potential investors or lenders.
7. **Create a Roadmap:** With a business plan, you have a roadmap that guides you in making key decisions and taking necessary actions to achieve your goals. It helps you stay organized and focused as you build your business.

Components of a Business Plan

While the structure of a business plan can vary, it generally includes the following components:

1. **Executive Summary:** This section provides an overview of your nutrition coaching business, including its mission, vision, and goals. It should capture the essence of your business and entice readers to learn more.
2. **Company Description:** Here, you detail the nature of your business, the services you offer, and your unique selling proposition. Explain what sets you apart from the competition.
3. **Market Analysis:** Conduct a comprehensive analysis of your target market, including demographics, trends, and competition. Identify your ideal customers and their needs, and explain how you will meet those needs.
4. **Organization and Management:** Describe the structure of your business, including the roles and responsibilities of key team members. Discuss any strategic partnerships or collaborations that will help your business thrive.
5. **Marketing and Sales Strategies:** Outline your marketing and sales efforts, including your pricing strategy, advertising methods, and plans to attract and retain clients. Detail how you will promote your services and grow your client base.
6. **Product and Service Line:** Provide detailed information about the nutrition

coaching services you offer, including any specialty areas or programs. Explain the benefits and outcomes clients can expect.
7. **Operational Plan:** Explain how your business will function day-to-day, including office location, equipment, staffing, and administrative processes. Ensure you have a solid plan for managing your operations smoothly.
8. **Financial Projections:** Present your financial forecasts, including startup costs, operating expenses, revenue projections, and break-even analysis. These projections should be based on thorough research and realistic assumptions.
9. **Funding Request:** If you require funding, outline the amount you are seeking and how the funds will be used. Be clear and specific about your financial needs and how the investment will help your business grow.
10. **Appendix:** Include any additional supporting documents such as market research data, certifications, or resumes of key team members. This section provides extra context and credibility to your business plan.

Tips for Developing an Effective Business Plan

1. **Research Extensively:** Gather as much information as possible about the nutrition coaching industry, market trends, and your competition. Use this knowledge to inform

your business plan and ensure it's grounded in reality.
2. **Be Realistic:** Set realistic goals and financial projections based on careful analysis and research. Avoid making overly optimistic assumptions that could set you up for disappointment.
3. **Seek Professional Help:** If you're unfamiliar with business planning, consider seeking guidance from a business consultant or mentor. They can provide valuable insights and help you avoid common pitfalls.
4. **Update Regularly:** Your business plan should be a living document that evolves as your business grows. Review and update it regularly to stay aligned with your goals and changing market conditions.
5. **Be Concise:** While it's essential to provide detailed information, remember to keep your business plan concise and reader-friendly. Use charts, graphs, and bullet points to convey information effectively and make it easy to understand.

Developing a comprehensive and well-thought-out business plan lays the foundation for your nutrition coaching business. Spend adequate time and effort on this crucial step to set yourself up for long-term success. In the next chapter, we will discuss the legal and regulatory considerations when starting your business.

Chapter 5: Legal and Regulatory Considerations

Embarking on the journey to start your own nutrition coaching business is exciting, but it comes with its own set of responsibilities, especially when it comes to legal and regulatory considerations. Understanding these aspects is crucial to ensure you run your business smoothly and stay on the right side of the law. Let's delve into the essential legal and regulatory elements you need to be aware of.

Licensing and Certification

While there's no specific license required to become a nutrition coach, obtaining certain certifications can greatly enhance your credibility and attract more clients. Think about getting certifications from reputable organizations like the National Academy of Sports Medicine (NASM) or the International Society of Sports Nutrition (ISSN). These certifications not only boost your credibility but also demonstrate your commitment to professional standards.

Moreover, it's important to stay informed about the regulations and requirements in your specific location. Some states or countries may have particular licensing requirements or regulations for nutrition coaches. Doing your homework to research and comply with any applicable laws can save you from potential legal headaches down the line.

Insurance Coverage

Insurance coverage might not be legally mandated, but it's a smart move to protect your business from potential liabilities. Imagine the peace of mind that comes with knowing you're covered in case of accidents or unforeseen circumstances. Consider securing professional liability insurance, general liability insurance, and cyber liability insurance to cover various risks that may arise. It's wise to consult with an insurance agent or broker who specializes in small businesses to find the most suitable coverage for your needs.

Data Protection and Privacy

As a nutrition coach, you'll be handling personal information from your clients, including their health history and dietary preferences. Protecting this sensitive data is paramount. Familiarize yourself with data protection laws, such as the General Data Protection Regulation (GDPR) if you have clients in the European Union. Implement secure methods for data storage and ensure you have appropriate consent forms for collecting and using personal information. By prioritizing data protection, you build trust with your clients and safeguard your business.

Business Structure and Tax Obligations

Choosing the right business structure is a key decision for both legal and tax purposes. Common structures for nutrition coaching businesses include sole proprietorship, partnership, limited liability company (LLC), or corporation. Each comes with its own set of advantages and disadvantages, so consulting with a legal professional or accountant is essential to determine the best fit for your business.

Understanding your tax obligations is equally important. Register your business with the appropriate tax authorities, obtain any necessary tax identification numbers, and familiarize yourself with the tax laws that apply to your business. Hiring an accountant can be incredibly beneficial in navigating the complexities of business taxes and ensuring compliance, giving you more time to focus on your clients.

Compliance with Advertising and Marketing Laws

Promoting your nutrition coaching services is crucial, but it's important to do so ethically and legally. Avoid making false or misleading claims about your services, and refrain from using testimonials or before-and-after photos without proper consent. Familiarize yourself with the regulations set by advertising and marketing governing bodies in your country or region. For instance, in the United States, the Federal Trade Commission (FTC) has guidelines for truth in advertising. Ensuring all your marketing materials, including your website and social media content, adhere to these guidelines helps you build a reputable and trustworthy business.

Conclusion

Understanding the legal and regulatory considerations of starting a nutrition coaching business is essential for operating ethically and in compliance with the law. Seeking professional advice when needed and staying informed about any changes in regulations will help you navigate the legal landscape and build a successful and reputable business. In the following chapters, we'll explore other crucial aspects of setting up and growing your nutrition coaching business. Stay tuned as we dive deeper into the journey of becoming a successful nutrition coach.

Chapter 6: Setting Up Your Business Operations

Setting up your business operations is a crucial step in starting a nutrition coaching business. It involves establishing the necessary systems and processes to ensure the smooth running of your business. This chapter will guide you through the key considerations and steps involved in setting up your business operations.

Determine Your Business Structure

The first step in setting up your business operations is determining the legal structure of your business. There are different options to choose from, including sole proprietorship, partnership, limited liability company (LLC), or corporation. Each structure has its own advantages and disadvantages in terms of liability, tax obligations, and flexibility. Consider consulting with a business attorney or tax professional to determine the most suitable structure for your nutrition coaching business. They can help you understand the legal and financial implications of each option and assist you in meeting the necessary requirements and filings.

Obtain Necessary Licenses and Permits

Depending on your location, you may be required to obtain certain licenses and permits to legally operate your nutrition coaching business. Research the local regulations and requirements to ensure compliance. Common licenses and permits may include health and safety permits, business operation licenses, and professional certifications. It is essential to stay updated on any changes in regulations and maintain proper documentation to avoid any legal issues in the future.

Set Up Your Workspace

Setting up a dedicated workspace for your nutrition coaching business is important for efficiency and professionalism. Consider whether you will be running your business from a home office or renting a separate space. If you choose to work from home, create a designated area that is free from distractions and conducive to productivity. Set up a desk, comfortable seating, and any necessary equipment or tools such as a computer, printer, and phone. If you decide to rent a separate workspace, ensure it meets your specific requirements. Consider factors such as location, accessibility, and cost. You may also need to arrange for utilities, internet, and other amenities to support your business operations.

Establish Financial Systems

Establishing financial systems is crucial for any business. It helps you keep track of your income, expenses, and profitability. Consider the following steps when setting up your financial systems:

- **Open a separate business bank account:** This will help you separate your personal and business finances, making it easier to track income and expenses.
- **Implement an accounting system:** Choose an accounting software that suits your needs and helps you manage invoicing, receipts, and financial reports. Popular options include QuickBooks and Xero.
- **Set up invoicing and payment processing:** Create a system for generating and sending invoices to clients. Consider using online payment platforms for convenient and secure transactions.
- **Track expenses:** Keep detailed records of your business expenses, including receipts and invoices. This will help you accurately calculate your tax deductions and monitor your cash flow.

Develop Administrative Processes

Developing efficient administrative processes is essential for managing your nutrition coaching business smoothly. Consider the following aspects:

- **Client onboarding:** Create a streamlined process for onboarding new clients, which includes collecting necessary information, obtaining signed agreements, and setting expectations.
- **Appointment scheduling:** Utilize scheduling software or online calendar tools to manage your appointments and ensure proper time management.
- **Document management:** Establish a system for organizing and storing client documents securely. This may include intake forms, progress reports, and personalized nutrition plans.
- **Communication channels:** Determine the primary channels through which you will communicate with your clients, such as email, phone, or video conferencing. Set clear guidelines for response times and preferred methods of communication.

Consider Hiring Support Staff

As your nutrition coaching business grows, you may consider hiring support staff to help with administrative tasks, marketing, or client management. Assess your workload and determine which areas would benefit from additional assistance. Hiring support staff can help you focus on coaching and growing your business, while delegating routine tasks to others. Consider outsourcing certain tasks or hiring part-time employees or virtual assistants to manage specific responsibilities.

Conclusion

Setting up your business operations is a critical step in starting a successful nutrition coaching business. By determining your business structure, obtaining necessary licenses, setting up your workspace, establishing financial systems, developing administrative processes, and considering hiring support staff, you can ensure the smooth running of your business. Taking these steps will provide a solid foundation for growth and enable you to focus on delivering exceptional nutrition coaching services to your clients.

Let's delve into each section a bit more deeply:

Determining Your Business Structure

When choosing the legal structure for your nutrition coaching business, it's important to weigh your options carefully. Each business structure has unique implications for liability, taxes, and overall flexibility. Here's a brief overview of the common structures:

- **Sole Proprietorship:** This is the simplest form of business structure, where you, as the owner, are personally responsible for all the business's debts and obligations. It's easy to set up and gives you complete control, but it doesn't offer any personal liability protection.
- **Partnership:** If you're starting your business with one or more partners, a

partnership might be a good option. In a partnership, each partner contributes to the business and shares in the profits and losses. However, like a sole proprietorship, partners are personally liable for the business's obligations.

- **Limited Liability Company (LLC):** An LLC offers more flexibility and protection. It separates your personal assets from your business assets, which means you're not personally liable for business debts. This structure combines the benefits of a corporation (liability protection) with those of a partnership (flexibility).
- **Corporation:** A corporation is a more complex structure, often suitable for larger businesses. It provides the most liability protection, as the business is considered a separate legal entity. However, it requires more paperwork and comes with more regulations and tax requirements.

To make the best decision, it's wise to consult with a business attorney or tax professional. They can provide detailed advice based on your specific situation and help you understand the legal and financial implications of each structure.

Obtaining Necessary Licenses and Permits

Operating legally is crucial, and obtaining the right licenses and permits is part of that process. The requirements can vary widely depending on your location, so it's essential to do your homework.

Here are some common licenses and permits you might need:

- **Health and Safety Permits:** These ensure that your business complies with local health and safety regulations, which is particularly important if you're giving dietary advice or handling food products.
- **Business Operation License:** This general license allows you to legally operate your business within a specific jurisdiction.
- **Professional Certifications:** Some areas require specific certifications for nutrition coaches. Check with local regulatory bodies to ensure you meet all necessary requirements.

Staying updated on regulations is also important, as laws can change. Keeping proper documentation is vital to avoid any legal issues down the line.

Setting Up Your Workspace

Your workspace is more than just a place to work; it's a reflection of your professionalism and efficiency. Whether you choose to work from home or rent an office, your workspace should be conducive to productivity.

- **Home Office:** If you're working from home, designate a specific area for your business. This helps create a clear boundary between your work and personal life. Equip your office with a good desk, comfortable seating, and necessary tools

like a computer, printer, and phone. Ensure the area is quiet and free from distractions.
- **Rented Office Space:** If you opt for a rented space, choose a location that's convenient for both you and your clients. Consider the cost, accessibility, and any amenities you might need. Make sure the space meets your professional needs and creates a welcoming environment for your clients.

Establishing Financial Systems

Financial management is a cornerstone of any successful business. Setting up robust financial systems helps you keep track of your income, expenses, and overall profitability. Here's how you can get started:

- **Open a Separate Business Bank Account:** This helps keep your personal and business finances separate, making it easier to manage your money and track your business's financial health.
- **Implement an Accounting System:** Choose accounting software that fits your needs. Popular options like QuickBooks and Xero offer tools for managing invoices, receipts, and financial reports.
- **Set Up Invoicing and Payment Processing:** Develop a system for creating and sending invoices to clients. Online payment platforms can streamline transactions and provide secure payment options for your clients.

- **Track Expenses:** Keeping detailed records of all your business expenses is crucial. This not only helps with tax deductions but also provides a clear picture of your cash flow.

Developing Administrative Processes

Efficient administrative processes are essential for running your nutrition coaching business smoothly. Here are some key areas to focus on:

- **Client Onboarding:** Develop a clear process for bringing new clients on board. This should include collecting necessary information, obtaining signed agreements, and setting clear expectations.
- **Appointment Scheduling:** Use scheduling software or online calendar tools to manage your appointments. This helps ensure you're making the best use of your time and avoiding scheduling conflicts.
- **Document Management:** Create a system for organizing and securely storing client documents. This might include intake forms, progress reports, and personalized nutrition plans.
- **Communication Channels:** Decide how you will communicate with your clients, whether it's via email, phone, or video conferencing. Set clear guidelines for response times and preferred communication methods.

Considering Hiring Support Staff

As your business grows, you might find that you need help managing administrative tasks, marketing, or client management. Assess your workload and identify areas where additional assistance could be beneficial. Hiring support staff can free up your time to focus on coaching and expanding your business.

- **Outsourcing:** Consider outsourcing specific tasks to freelancers or virtual assistants. This can be a cost-effective way to get the help you need without the commitment of hiring full-time employees.
- **Part-Time Employees:** If you need more consistent support, hiring part-time staff can be a great option. They can help with routine tasks and allow you to concentrate on higher-level activities.

Conclusion

Setting up your business operations is a critical step in starting a successful nutrition coaching business. By determining your business structure, obtaining necessary licenses, setting up your workspace, establishing financial systems, developing administrative processes, and considering hiring support staff, you can ensure the smooth running of your business. Taking these steps will provide a solid foundation for growth and enable you to focus on delivering exceptional nutrition coaching services to your clients.

Chapter 7: Building Your Brand and Online Presence

Hey there! Let's dive into something super important for your nutrition coaching business: building a strong brand and establishing a solid online presence. Trust me, these steps are crucial for standing out from the competition, attracting your target audience, and reaching a wider crowd. Plus, it helps you build credibility in the industry. So, let's explore some strategies and techniques to build your brand and create a strong online presence.

Defining Your Brand

Before you start building your brand, it's essential to define your unique value proposition and clearly identify your target audience. Your brand should reflect your business values, personality, and the benefits you offer to your clients. Think of it as your business's personality. To get started, ask yourself these questions:

- What makes your nutrition coaching business unique?
- What are your core values and beliefs?
- What are the main problems or challenges faced by your target audience?
- How can you position yourself as the solution to these problems?

Once you have a clear understanding of your brand, you can start developing a consistent brand identity across all your marketing channels.

Creating a Brand Identity

Your brand identity includes all the visual elements and messaging associated with your business. This encompasses your logo, color palette, typography, and tone of voice. Consistency is key here because it helps build recognition and trust among your target audience.

Start by designing a professional logo that represents your brand. Keep it simple, memorable, and visually appealing. Next, choose colors that align with your brand personality and evoke the desired emotions from your audience. Pick fonts that are easy to read and reflect the tone of your brand.

In addition to your logo, create branded templates for your marketing materials. This includes social media graphics, newsletters, and blog posts. Make sure these templates follow your brand guidelines and maintain a consistent look and feel. This consistency helps your audience recognize your content instantly.

Building an Engaging Website

Think of your website as the virtual storefront of your nutrition coaching business. It plays a crucial role in building your online presence. Your website should not only look good but also provide valuable information to your visitors.

Start by selecting a reliable hosting provider and choose a content management system (CMS) that suits your needs. WordPress is a popular choice for building websites because it offers a wide range of customization options.

When designing your website, keep these tips in mind:

- Use high-quality images that represent your brand and the positive outcomes of your services.
- Create clear and concise content that communicates your unique value proposition and resonates with your target audience.
- Optimize your website for search engines by incorporating relevant keywords in your content and meta tags.
- Make it easy for visitors to navigate your website and find the information they're looking for.
- Include testimonials and success stories from satisfied clients to build trust and credibility.

Utilizing Social Media

Social media platforms are powerful tools for building your online presence and engaging with your audience. Choose the platforms that are most popular among your target audience and focus your efforts on those channels. Create a social media content strategy that aligns with your brand and business goals.

Post regularly and consistently to keep your audience engaged. Share valuable tips, recipes, and success stories related to nutrition coaching. Encourage your followers to engage with your content by asking questions and starting conversations. Use social media to showcase your expertise by sharing educational content and participating in relevant discussions.

Engage with your followers by responding to their comments and messages promptly. Building relationships and connections on social media can lead to valuable client referrals and partnerships.

Networking and Collaboration

Networking and collaborating with other professionals in the health and wellness industry can help expand your reach and establish your expertise. Attend industry conferences, workshops, and events to meet like-minded professionals and potential clients.

Collaborate with complementary businesses, such as fitness trainers or wellness centers, to cross-promote each other's services. Consider partnering with influencers or bloggers in the nutrition and wellness niche. Their endorsement and support can significantly increase your online visibility and credibility.

Guest blogging or appearing as a guest on podcasts or webinars can also help you reach a wider audience and position yourself as an expert in your field.

Monitoring and Adjusting

Building a brand and online presence is an ongoing process. It's important to monitor your efforts and adjust your strategy as needed. Use website analytics and social media insights to track the performance of your marketing efforts. Identify what is working well and what can be improved.

Stay up to date with the latest trends in digital marketing to ensure that your brand remains relevant and competitive. Being flexible and willing to adapt will keep you ahead of the game.

Conclusion

Building your brand and establishing a strong online presence are crucial steps in growing your nutrition coaching business. By defining your brand, creating a brand identity, building an engaging website, utilizing social media, networking and collaborating, and monitoring and adjusting your efforts, you can attract your target audience, build credibility, and achieve long-term success in the industry. So, get out there and start building your brand—you've got this!

Chapter 8: Acquiring Clients and Networking

Acquiring clients and building a strong network is essential for the success of your nutrition coaching business. Think of it as laying the foundation for your growth and sustainability. In this chapter, we'll explore effective strategies to attract clients and establish valuable connections within the health and wellness industry.

Identifying Your Ideal Client

Before you can effectively acquire clients, it's crucial to identify who your ideal client is. Take some time to think about the demographic characteristics, goals, and challenges of the clients you want to work with. By understanding your target market, you can tailor your marketing messages to resonate with their needs and interests.

Consider conducting market research, surveys, or interviews to gain insights into your potential clients' preferences, pain points, and motivations. This information is invaluable as it helps you refine your marketing strategies and develop a compelling message that attracts your ideal clients.

Creating a Compelling Marketing Message

Once you have a clear picture of your ideal client, it's time to create a compelling marketing message that speaks directly to them. Your marketing message should clearly communicate the unique value and benefits you offer as a nutrition coach.

Start by identifying the main problem or challenge your ideal client faces. Then, highlight how your services can help solve that problem or address their needs. Make sure to emphasize the benefits and outcomes clients can expect from working with you, such as improved health, increased energy, or weight loss.

Crafting a powerful marketing message requires a deep understanding of your target market's pain points and desires. Use language that speaks directly to your clients and evokes emotions. Avoid using jargon or complex terminology that might confuse or alienate potential clients. Keep it simple, clear, and impactful.

Leveraging Online Marketing

In today's digital age, online marketing is a powerful tool for acquiring clients and establishing your presence in the nutrition coaching industry. Here are some effective online marketing strategies to consider:

1. **Website Optimization:** Ensure that your website is user-friendly, visually appealing,

and optimized for search engines. Use strategic keywords related to nutrition coaching throughout your website to improve your ranking in search engine results.
2. **Content Marketing:** Create valuable and informative content that showcases your expertise and helps your target audience. This can include blog posts, articles, videos, or podcasts. Share your content on your website, social media platforms, and other relevant online platforms to attract and engage potential clients.
3. **Social Media Marketing:** Leverage the power of social media platforms like Facebook, Instagram, and LinkedIn to connect with your audience, share valuable content, and build brand awareness. Engage with your followers, respond to comments, and foster relationships with potential clients.
4. **Email Marketing:** Build an email list of interested prospects and regularly send them valuable content, tips, recipes, and special offers. This will help you stay connected with your audience and nurture relationships, ultimately leading to client conversions.
5. **Online Advertising:** Consider utilizing online advertising platforms like Google AdWords or Facebook Ads to reach a wider audience and promote your services. Target your ads to specific demographics or geographic regions to maximize their effectiveness.

Networking and Collaborating

Networking and collaborating with professionals in the health and wellness industry can be an effective way to acquire clients and expand your reach. Here are some strategies to help you build valuable relationships:

1. **Join Professional Associations:** Consider joining professional associations or organizations related to nutrition, health coaching, or wellness. These groups often host networking events, conferences, and workshops where you can connect with like-minded professionals and potential clients.
2. **Attend Industry Conferences and Workshops:** Participate in industry conferences, workshops, and seminars to stay up to date with the latest trends and research in nutrition coaching. These events provide opportunities to meet industry experts, potential clients, and potential collaborators.
3. **Collaborate with Complementary Professionals:** Identify complementary professionals, such as personal trainers, doctors, or yoga instructors, and explore ways to collaborate. For example, you could offer joint workshops or referral partnerships to mutually benefit each other's businesses.
4. **Offer Educational Workshops and Webinars:** Host educational workshops or webinars on relevant nutrition topics to showcase your expertise and attract potential clients. Promote these events

through your website, social media, and email marketing to reach a wider audience.

5. **Participate in Online Communities:** Engage with online communities and forums related to nutrition and wellness. Be helpful, provide valuable insights, and establish yourself as an authority in the field. This can help you attract potential clients who are seeking guidance and support.

By implementing these strategies, you can effectively acquire clients and expand your network within the nutrition coaching industry. Remember to consistently evaluate and adjust your marketing efforts based on feedback and insights to ensure long-term success. Keep building those connections and refining your approach, and you'll see your business grow and thrive.

Chapter 9: Providing Exceptional Service

As a nutrition coach, delivering exceptional service to your clients is key to building a successful business and establishing a stellar reputation in the industry. When you provide outstanding care and support, you help your clients reach their health and wellness goals, increasing their satisfaction and loyalty. Let's dive into what it takes to offer exceptional service as a nutrition coach.

Understanding Client Needs and Goals

To truly provide exceptional service, you need to get to the heart of your client's unique needs and goals. Start by listening actively. Ask detailed questions to uncover insights into their dietary preferences, lifestyle, medical conditions, and desired outcomes. By gathering this information, you can tailor your nutrition coaching services to each individual, creating personalized plans that are practical, realistic, and sustainable.

Think of it like this: Each client is on their own health journey, and your job is to walk alongside them, offering guidance that's perfectly suited to their path. This personalized approach not only shows that you care but also helps your clients see better results.

Developing Personalized Nutrition Plans

Once you have a clear understanding of your client's needs and goals, it's time to develop personalized nutrition plans. These plans should be effective and flexible, considering food preferences, cultural background, allergies or intolerances, and any medical conditions. Aim to create balanced and varied eating plans that meet nutritional requirements while fitting into the client's life seamlessly.

Remember, the goal is to make healthy eating enjoyable and sustainable. By taking into account individual circumstances, you ensure that the nutrition plans you develop are not just about following a diet but about making a lasting lifestyle change.

Providing Education and Guidance

As a nutrition coach, one of your primary roles is to educate and empower your clients to make informed decisions about their nutrition and overall health. Share your knowledge about different food groups, portion control, meal planning, and the benefits of a balanced diet. Teach them how to read food labels and make healthier choices when dining out.

Offer practical tips on grocery shopping, cooking techniques, and meal preparation to make healthy eating more convenient and enjoyable. The more informed your clients are, the more confident they'll feel in making positive changes to their diet and lifestyle.

Offering Ongoing Support and Motivation

To keep your clients committed to their nutrition goals, it's essential to offer ongoing support and motivation. Regular check-ins, whether in person, over the phone, or via email, allow you to monitor progress, address challenges, and celebrate achievements.

Encouragement and praise go a long way in keeping clients motivated. Offer constructive feedback and provide resources like recipes, meal plans, and educational materials to help them stay on track even between coaching sessions. Your consistent support helps clients stay focused and driven towards their health goals.

Continued Professional Development

In the ever-evolving field of nutrition, staying updated on the latest research, trends, and best practices is crucial. Continuous professional development allows you to enhance your knowledge and skills, ensuring your services are evidence-based and up-to-date.

Attend conferences, webinars, workshops, and seminars. Seek out opportunities for networking and collaboration with other health and wellness professionals. By continuously learning, you not only improve your expertise but also demonstrate your commitment to providing the best possible service to your clients.

Soliciting and Incorporating Client Feedback

Client feedback is invaluable for improving and refining your nutrition coaching services. Actively seek feedback through satisfaction surveys, one-on-one check-ins, or online reviews. Pay attention to their suggestions and incorporate them into your practice wherever possible.

By continually striving for improvement based on client feedback, you can consistently enhance the quality of your service and exceed client expectations. This not only helps you grow as a professional but also strengthens your relationship with your clients.

Conclusion

Providing exceptional service is more than a professional obligation; it's a reflection of your passion and commitment to helping others achieve optimal health and wellness through nutrition. By understanding and addressing your clients' needs, developing personalized nutrition plans, offering ongoing support and education, and continuously seeking professional development, you can set yourself apart as a trusted and exceptional nutrition coach.

Your dedication to providing exceptional service will not only help your clients succeed but also establish your reputation as a leader in the field of nutrition coaching. So, take these principles to heart and watch your business thrive as you help your clients transform their lives for the better.

Chapter 10: Growing Your Nutrition Coaching Business

As a nutrition coach, your ultimate goal is to grow your business and expand your reach. This chapter will provide you with valuable insights and strategies to drive growth and take your nutrition coaching business to the next level.

1. Enhance Your Marketing Efforts

To attract more clients and grow your nutrition coaching business, it's crucial to have a strong marketing strategy. Here are some tips to enhance your marketing efforts:

Identify and Target New Markets

Think about expanding your target market to reach a wider audience. Identify niche markets or specific demographics that could benefit from your unique services. Conduct thorough market research to understand their needs and preferences, and then tailor your marketing messages accordingly.

Utilize Social Media Marketing

Social media platforms are powerful tools for reaching and engaging with your target audience. Create compelling content that provides valuable information, tips, and advice. Use platforms like Facebook, Instagram, and LinkedIn to connect with potential clients, share success stories, and promote your services. Regularly post engaging content, such as client testimonials, nutrition tips, and behind-the-scenes looks at your coaching process.

Optimize Your Website for Search Engines

Make sure your website is search engine optimized (SEO) so potential clients can easily find you online. Research and implement relevant keywords, create informative content, and improve your website's loading speed and user experience. A well-optimized website not only attracts more visitors but also enhances your credibility and professionalism.

Invest in Online Advertising

Consider investing in paid online advertising to boost your visibility and attract more clients. Platforms like Google AdWords and Facebook Ads allow you to target specific demographics and reach a wider audience. Set a budget for online advertising and monitor your campaigns to ensure you're getting a good return on investment.

2. Develop Partnerships and Collaborations

Collaborating with other professionals and businesses in the health and wellness industry can significantly benefit your nutrition coaching business.

Build Referral Networks

Establish relationships with healthcare providers, fitness centers, gyms, and other professionals who cater to individuals seeking improved health and nutrition. Offer to provide educational workshops or guest blog posts to showcase your expertise and attract potential clients. Building a strong referral network can lead to a steady stream of new clients.

Create Joint Ventures

Partner with complementary professionals, such as personal trainers, yoga instructors, or therapists, to offer bundled services or joint programs. This not only expands your reach but also provides added value to your clients. Joint ventures can help you tap into new client bases and create innovative, comprehensive health and wellness solutions.

Attend Industry Conferences and Events

Networking is vital for growing your business. Attend conferences, workshops, and seminars in the health and wellness industry to connect with like-minded professionals, stay updated on industry trends, and potentially gain new clients. These events provide opportunities to showcase your expertise and learn from others in your field.

3. Leverage the Power of Testimonials

Testimonials and success stories from satisfied clients can significantly boost your credibility and attract new clients. Encourage your current clients to provide testimonials and share their success stories with others.

Showcase Testimonials on Your Website and Social Media

Display testimonials prominently on your website and share them on your social media platforms. This allows potential clients to see the positive impact you've had on others and instills confidence in your services. A well-placed testimonial can be the deciding factor for someone considering your services.

Create Case Studies

Develop case studies that highlight the specific challenges your clients faced and the positive outcomes they achieved through your coaching. Use these case studies to demonstrate your expertise and success rate. Detailed case studies can provide potential clients with a clear picture of how you can help them achieve their goals.

Request Online Reviews

Ask your satisfied clients to leave reviews on popular review platforms like Google My Business, Yelp, or Facebook. Positive reviews can greatly influence potential clients' decision-making process and improve your online reputation. Respond to reviews, both positive and negative, to show that you value client feedback and are committed to improving your services.

4. Expand Your Service Offerings

Consider expanding your service offerings to further meet the needs of your clients and attract new ones. Here are some ideas to diversify your services:

Group Coaching Programs

Develop group coaching programs to cater to clients who prefer a supportive and collaborative environment. Group programs can also be more cost-effective for clients and allow you to reach a larger audience. Group sessions can foster a sense of community and provide clients with additional motivation and support.

Online Courses or E-Books

Create online courses or e-books that provide in-depth nutritional information and guidance. This allows you to reach a broader audience beyond your local area and provides an additional income stream. Online courses and e-books can be sold through your website, providing a passive income source while expanding your reach.

Workshops and Seminars

Host workshops and seminars on specific topics related to nutrition and wellness. These events not only position you as an expert but also allow you to connect with potential clients directly. Workshops and seminars can be held in-person or online, giving you flexibility in how you reach your audience.

5. Continuously Improve Yourself and Your Services

Never stop learning and growing as a nutrition coach. Continuously seek opportunities for personal and professional development to enhance your skills and knowledge. Here are some ways to achieve this:

Attend Industry Conferences and Workshops

Stay updated on the latest research, trends, and advancements in nutrition coaching by attending industry conferences and workshops. These events provide valuable insights and networking opportunities. Regular attendance at such events ensures you stay at the forefront of your field.

Pursue Advanced Certifications

Consider pursuing advanced certifications or specialized training to expand your expertise in specific areas of nutrition coaching. This can further differentiate you from competitors and attract clients with specific needs. Advanced certifications can enhance your credibility and open up new opportunities for growth.

Engage in Continuous Education

Stay informed about the latest research, studies, and best practices in nutrition coaching through continuous education. Read books, scientific papers, and reputable websites to deepen your understanding and improve your practice. Make learning a lifelong commitment to ensure you provide the best possible service to your clients.

Seek Feedback and Implement Improvements

Regularly seek feedback from your clients to understand their needs and preferences. Make necessary adjustments to your coaching approach, programs, and services based on the feedback to consistently provide exceptional value to your clients. By listening to your clients and making improvements, you can ensure high client satisfaction and retention.

By implementing these strategies and continuously improving your services, you can effectively grow your nutrition coaching business and help more individuals achieve their health and wellness goals. Now that you have learned how to grow your nutrition coaching business, you have the tools and knowledge to take your business to new heights. The next chapter will conclude this book and provide final thoughts and tips for long-term success.

Growing your nutrition coaching business is an ongoing process that requires dedication, creativity, and a willingness to adapt. By enhancing your marketing efforts, developing partnerships, leveraging testimonials, expanding your service offerings, and continuously improving yourself and your services, you can build a thriving business that helps more people achieve their health and wellness goals. Remember, the journey to success is a marathon, not a sprint, so stay focused, keep learning, and enjoy the process.

www.ingramcontent.com/pod-product-compliance
Lightning Source LLC
Chambersburg PA
CBHW070129230526
45472CB00004B/1494